Something You Didn't Know

Jaruby Jazmin

BookLeaf
Publishing

India | USA | UK

Presentation by *BookLeaf Publishing*

Web: www.bookleafpub.com

E-mail: info@bookleafpub.com

ISBN: 9789358315738

First edition 2023

*This book is dedicated to those who know me,
in hopes of helping you understand the soul
behind the smile.*

*It is also written for anyone that may find
solace in my words; comfort by companionship,
if not by memory.*

PREFACE

Before you read this, please be aware some of these works were written more than 7 years time. Some have been collecting dust or tucked away in digital drawer. Many published works no longer align by my current thoughts, feelings, or beliefs, but were published for their beauty and for their charm. I hope you can understand me by reading these few letters that took place at different times.

One

All the other places in the world to end up and
you ended up here,
As a collective whole or as a bittersweet
surprise.

There's nothing pure anymore.

Everything's mixed.
Everything's tainted.

Maybe that's why I try to numb myself with
mixed drinks, with drugs, with impersonal
relationships.
Fake stories, fake laughs, fake memories.

Maybe we're all just pretending.
Maybe we're all just the same.

And usually writing helps, but not when it's this
messy.
This is just my life on paper.
And the only difference is that I can burn this
one.

You'd think I'd know how to do this by now.

Deal with all the anger, the jealousy, the madness and the sadness.

But all I can do is nothing at all.

Two

Maybe I don't want to be helped, but I don't
want to stay either.

Things make sense and yet, they don't.

Does anything really have a meaning anymore?

There's a special place in hell for people like me.
The victim, the murderer, the torturer, the vain,
the helpless, the young.

I'm just screaming out for attention.
But the thing is, nobody is close enough to hear.
Or they don't care.

Regardless, I still end up alone.
Something so sad and yet, so inevitable.

Maybe fill a few empty pages with nothing but
thoughts and bad memories.
But they can't stay in my head.

They can't.

Three

A clean sheet. Messy writing.
It's not my style, but it's what's left.
At least for now.

I try to avoid everything.
The thinking, the feeling, the waiting, the loving.
It seems so empty, so vague.

So I try to make the time go faster.
By sleeping, by eating, by doing a thousand
mindless acts and hoping for something,
Just a piece of something.

But it never comes, so why keep waiting?
In hopes that something great will come around?

Maybe that's why I've welcomed death into my
life.
Because I've come to realize that I have
absolutely no control over certain things, make
that most things actually.

I've made mistake after mistake and the end is
nowhere in sight,

But if you really knew, then maybe you'd reach
out.

For me..

Or for you.

Four

Do you feel the shame?
Like I do.

Because I never wanted to, but it happened
anyways.
And maybe it was meant to, but I never meant
for it to happen.
It doesn't matter anyways.

Disaster averted.
Well, different disaster.
You had your own.

Often I want to disappear.
But not from my life or from my job,
I want to disappear from my mind.
And be happy, be truly happy.
Not this happiness that I fake for others.
But then what good would any of it do?
And who'd know the difference?

Because I find comfort in the discomfort of it
all.
Because I find myself in the midst of chaos and
impurity.

But you're happy so I'll let you be
Because you could never be truly happy with
me.

Five

Page after page.
Mistake after mistake.
You can see the pattern setting in now, can't
you?

Because it's only crazy motherfuckers who could
align the chaos of the stars.

I overthink. It's true.
I can't be alone. That's also true.
I can't be by myself. I can't sleep. I hate sleeping
alone.
I hate the dark on the inside.
But it shines so beautifully outside.

I don't know what we're going to be, but I'd
rather not think about it.
I'd rather not make up daydreams and fairytales
about someone who could just as easily be gone.

It's funny,
You thought I was quick to leave,
But in reality,
You were the first to go.

And I'll find comfort in a stranger's arms,
Knowing that it's wrong
And wishing it was you.

But if I only have your memories
Then why can't I use them to pretend it's really
you

Six

And so the story goes.
Maybe not with the same characters, but with
the same author.

People think I'm crazy.
I think I'm just lost.
And I'll take direction from where it seems most
fun.

You're good at the meaningless conversations he
said.
All I said was I love you.
And I meant it.
And maybe now I regret it.
Just like I regret most things I've done.

I was stupid.
I was foolish.
I was young.

They talk of fools and kings, pawns and people;
But where does the line get drawn?
And if we're all getting used by each other
Then could we ever truly be loved by another?

I still think it's stupid of me to write like if
anyone actually gives a shit.
But it's what I do.
It's where I hide and at the same time, it's where
you can find me.

But only if you took the time to look.

Seven

You'd think I'd stop.
But the voices don't stop.
The thoughts keep pouring in
And they're not all that happy.

I think if I write enough, all of the bad thoughts
will eventually flow out and I'd have my mind
back.

But, for the time being,
You're on my mind.
And I can't go 30 seconds without thinking of
your face.

It's just hard to distinguish truth from emotion.
I wish you wouldn't decide things like that.
Emotions are so fickle.
And apparently, so are we.
What I would give just to be the way we were
before,
Happy.

But it's too late for something bright.
The only thing that awaits is the uncertainty and
loneliness.

The only thing that awaits is the darkness,
The one thing I'm scared of.

Eight

I've written so many pages and I still feel the same.
Because I hate the sound of love and I can't bear to see the bright side of this love.
Because I can't unsee it.
Because it's on the other side of the spectrum,
Between reality and possibility.
Because no matter how messy this gets,
It won't ever be clean
So add fuel to the flames.

Maybe you were expecting me to change for you.
I can't change.
I can't be someone I want even for the person I most want.

Maybe if you actually loved me, we wouldn't be here.
And I knew I shouldn't have believed you.
But you were so nice and sincere.

I always thought that if I went for the nice guy I wouldn't ever get hurt.

But life's a bitch, and the nicest guy I ever dated
broke my heart apart
Just like I had done many times before..

Nine

Should we keep going?
Would it matter anyway?

And I have so many questions
But you're all out of answers.
So should I keep doing this to myself?

Are you doing what I did so many times before?
Are you enjoying this like I once did.

Because I write to get rid of the bad feelings
But I look at you again, and they all come
rolling back out
Sort of like a game at a carnival
Where I'm all out of tries
But you put in one more token
Just to keep me on my high

And I would never wish you any harm
But sometimes,
I wouldn't wish you any happiness either.
Because if it's not with me, then it would just
hurt.

And I'd rather have you feeling monotone

Than have me feeling down and un-unique in
every way.

Because I showed you every part of my soul.
But just like the one before,
You broke it and left.

And it hurts to show someone your everything.
Because I gave you my all and it still wasn't
enough.

Ten

I'm troubled
I'm lost.

Mostly because I don't know where to go from
now.

I wouldn't trust again.
Especially not anytime soon.
But you always made me feel like I could.

Thing is, I don't even trust myself.
Yeah, maybe I don't have any faith,
But when it comes to love,
It's never worked out.

Art is different.
Over time, things connect. They heal.
They're obscure and they're beautiful.

Just like the portrait of a life.
Filled with pain because that's what we
remember most,
but also with hope, that over time, we will
understand.

Eleven

A clean page.
And I still wouldn't stop because I have to taint
you with life.

Emptiness is not alive.
Emptiness is the absence of life.

You need substance.
I need substance.
But not in that way.

I love words and words are there for me
But to call it a love affair would be accurate in
another way
It's not a reciprocating love
It's an unrequited love.

Because words hurt,
Because ink stains,
And because memories don't fade,
At least not the bad ones.

But what would my life be like if I had no pain?
If I had no love?

Maybe,
It'd be just the same.

Run On

I should stop playing the victim, correct?
I mean yes, I got hurt and after all this time, it
still hurts, but I hurt you too. Maybe even more
profoundly than I'll ever know.
And I apologize for giving you up.

I set you on a silver platter and sent you on your
way.
I was too hurt to see your pain. But I ended the
possibility time after time.
My friend said I should leave you alone. She's
right.

This has gotten pathetic.

Because it's been over a month and I still cry in
my truck, and every conversation I have reminds
me of you. And I keep trying to resurrect our
inside jokes with other people, but they don't
seem to get it.

And I don't get them.

I can't look at anyone's face the way I look at
yours.

Their face doesn't glow, and they don't have the correct trace, and their eyes aren't shiny like yours. And their heart isn't like yours! Not even close.

So I stay in place and I write, maybe even trying to relive my right.

But I threw you away and I didn't appreciate you. And I doubted you without good reason. I sent you off. I didn't reply when you said you loved me. I was too hurt.
But I acted strong and that was probably my greatest mistake: Not admitting that without you I'm weak, weak to my knees.

You're the type of happiness that brings pain.

All the pretty words and all the ugly thoughts dance around to await my final faults. I loved you completely. And now, I can't think of anything more beautiful than being loved by you.

Intrusive Thoughts

I'm just done with it all.

Often I think of how easy it would be.

It's such a thin wrist.
It wouldn't take much, but it would take all.

And these thoughts aren't me, but when the tears
are all out and the sobbing has stopped, a
clearing remains.

And it brings a very simple message.

Nothing.
Nothing at all.

I'm not going to do anything stupid. I already
have.
And if you ever get to see me for me, then I'm
sorry.

There's no more tears left.

It's just empty.

Eulogy

I lose sleep over you
You lose sleep over me

I'm alive in your dreams.
But, baby, I'm dying.
& dancing joyously to the tomb.

Welcome, Love!

Welcome death.

Nothing is yours,
Nothing is mine,
So infinity could be ours!

You make me sad
You make me blue

I don't want to be sad
I don't want to be dad.

When you bury me,
Paint me happy and blue.

Death is a dream.

And my dream has come true.

Birthday Cake

Piece of cake, you make me whole
Speak to me, I know you're dark
But you feel like home

I know you were beaten
I know you were beat
But you've never known defeat

Birthday Cake,
You were made to gleam
Dressed for the occasion
But you never make it past the first beat

Let these vultures prey on you
Hungry eyes adore you
You stand so beautiful
Unaware you're about to taste deceit

Birthday Cake,
You did not die by my hands
But you were cut by my hands
For everyone had to make you suffer
In order to taste you bittersweet

Birthday Cake,

You're still alive.
Is it so?
Your poor beating heart
Clinging to life when you were born to be cut.
And once you've been touched, you'll be thrown
out.

Birthday Cake,
I'm eating your soul;
Restless
Because you can't ever be whole.

Cosmic Blues

Love, you make me sad
Love, you remind me of dad

Born in the same season
Perhaps even in the same reason

Love, you confuse me
Love, you just used me

With you I saw constellations
But you can't bring consolation

Love, I can hear you
Love, I can feel you

Absent and invisible
Stay like this, invincible

Love, I fear I'm the future
Love, I fear you're a suture

Why add the poem?
Maybe I owe them

Love has no name

It doesn't exist

Love has no pain
It's always a list

Love has no end
It's always dismissed

Love can be bent
And more often missed

Love cannot end
But I fear, my love,
That this is the end.

Cognitive Behavioral Therapy

11/10/2020 10:50:28 AM

Question: How did your first therapy session go?
Answer: Therapy went well. Yes, I cried. I felt strange afterwards; felt like I was missing my entire left arm but it wasn't an alarming feeling. It felt empty, but it was a good empty like the beginning of a new life.

11/10/2020 10:59:37 AM

Question: Do you think therapy helped?
Answer: It did, a lot. I'm glad I finally went. I'm going next Monday as well and working out details later.

11/10/2020 11:02:11 AM

Question: Do you like your therapist?
Answer: It's quite inspiring just how much trust she evoked out of me. I guess that's just the dynamic experienced between a psychotherapist and a patient. I say "I guess" because I have nothing else to compare it to.

11/10/2020 11:11:18 AM

Question: So, your therapist helped you to trust?
Answer: The trust was there immediately.

11/10/2020 11:11:42 AM

Question: Did she help you open up by making you feel like you could trust her?
Answer: I opened up immediately; that's never happened before. It's like she knew exactly which heart string to touch to help me find the music in my agony, if that makes sense to you. She helped me find my way.
That's all I really needed to say about it, but thank you for asking. It helps me articulate my feelings better. I've found that I can express my thoughts in writing a lot more clearly than I could by bringing them to life through the spoken word.

11/10/2020 11:17:50 AM

Question: Did it feel like you were sharing your thoughts and feeling with a stranger?
Answer: No

11/10/2020 11:18:00 AM

Question: Did it feel like your therapist actually cared and genuinely wanted to help you?
Answer: Yes, like I was talking to someone who actually -could- help.

Usually when I talk to others about my problems, it's more to help them understand why I am acting the way I am acting, but, yesterday, it felt like I was talking about my problems, so that it could help ME understand why I acted the way I did and to help me see that I was not wrong by reacting the way I did. My dad was the adult.

In conclusion, she always seemed to take the thoughts right out of my mind, rather than the words right out of my mouth. This is because the words were non-existent, they had not been born yet; they were still innocent.

Words are just thoughts that grew up and found their voice. Many of my thoughts are too innocent to become words and I feel like that is why I struggle to voice my feelings, furthermore, why I struggle to stand up for myself.

That's what I've processed right now as I'm talking to you about the experience from yesterday and even now, it feels weird for me to share my feelings and my way of thinking with you because its so near to me. The thought of any slight rejection would hurt. I know you would never reject me but even if you were to misunderstand, or not understand at all, the feelings that I am trying to portray, then it'd make me feel out of place.

That last part I only say so that you could understand what goes on in my head and why many times I avoid talking to people about my real feelings. I don't want to shut you guys out, but if you cannot understand my feelings in the beautiful way they were meant to be understood, then again it would just make me feel out of place when I only wanted to be who I am.

My head hurts now, but thank you for letting me share my thoughts. I've never taken anyone inside my mind, mostly because I never knew how to get through there myself, but I've gotten to know a small entryway and that's what I've shared with you today.

S.I.

12/23/2020 3:42:39 PM

Question: Is it hard to talk about your downs
with a therapist?
Answer: No, I tell her and she guides me out of
confusion. She says I've lost touch with my
anger. It's the newest topic of exploration for us.

12/23/2020 3:44:34 PM

Question: Whenever you were having suicidal
thoughts or if you have them, do you tell her? Or
is that something that you don't talk about?
Answer: If it's a pressing issue then yes. Like
that time I was telling you I was feeling it again,
had I gone to therapy that day or anytime near
that day then yes I would've brought it up.
It's not very pressing for me since my thoughts
have always been close to that subject, but as
I've gotten older, I just fantasize about leaving,
but I know deep down I probably wouldn't do it.
I'd just cry in pain and seek God. Not sure if
that's too much information, but that's how it is
for me.

12/23/2020 3:48:46 PM

Question: So you mean your thoughts have always been suicidal therefore it's not as pressing as it was before?
Answer: I'm used to the thought popping up; it's not a big deal anymore. I can reject the thought, though, I do admit, it pops up like a dream. So I'm drawn to it, but I stay grounded.. for family, for responsibility and for God. I know suicide is not the way.

12/23/2020 3:52:05 PM

Question: Why do you think it pops up every here and there?
Answer: It's the peace that calls me. The idea of rest. For everything to stop. To transcend. To leave and go on to the next adventure, if any. To finally talk to God, but I still fear because I wouldn't be admitted to heaven if I were to commit suicide.

12/23/2020 3:53:12 PM

Question: Do you believe you'd be sent to hell if you actually were to commit suicide?

Answer: Hell doesn't exist. God is not mean
enough to condemn anyone to hell. Your soul
would just cease to exist.

12/23/2020 3:53:47 PM
Question: You mean you want to die, but you
don't want to commit the act of suicide?
Answer: Yes, the gift of death.. from God. That's
what I many times long for, for him to bring me
back home. I'm weary from this Earth, but as
long as I'm here I have to believe there's many
reasons for it.
So I try to be nice, to be helpful, to give gifts
and give joy, to lessen the burden of others or to
make the world better since I know how dark it
can be. I feel like a martyr sometimes and I
know its not right. That's why I want to learn
more about God, because there's a certain way
we should be and certain boundaries that have to
be upheld. Maybe I feel shame and guilt and so I
overcompensate.
I'm straightening out my way of thinking, at
least I know what I think now. Before it all just
blurred with reality, but now I realize I see the
world a bit distorted and yes, my therapist is
helping me see those distortions.

Manslaughter

Let me maybe write.

About my dream from last night, or nightmare. It was odd.

My sister and I were in my childhood babysitter's husband's room, alone. With a bigger, heavier man than my dad, but his face was very very similar to that of my dad's. It could've been my dad's brother, if he ever had one.

Anyways, it seemed that he was intending on molesting or raping us. No words had been said by him to this intent, but I knew.

I felt scared, alarmed, trapped, panicked and without air.

I tried to yell for help or maybe even make a frightening noise to tell him, "Don't even try," but all I could gather was a squeak. A half or a quarter of a letter.

I tried again, knowing that my dad was in the
other room and could come to my rescue if he
could hear.

Two third's of a word formulated. I can do this.

I was so afraid. The man started to try and grab
my legs. I had a mechanical pencil in my hand
and scratched his arm with it as he tried again
and again.

I kept trying to use my voice, but it wasn't
coming along. I was afraid. I think I managed to
say "Pa!" but though the word came out, the
volume didn't. It sounded so low. He could've
only heard that cry for help if he was already in
the room.

I was so disappointed in myself.

There I was, in danger, real danger and I can
barely manage one abbreviated word at "indoor
voice" volume?

At that moment, I didn't think I could really call
for help, but that didn't stop me from trying. The
shirtless, overweight, pseudo-uncle didn't stop
trying either.

I felt my life was in danger.

I realized gouging his arm was not working and when his face got close I went for his eye. I aimed and at first, I'm not sure if I hit it, but in a quick second I had another chance. I stabbed his eye this time. I knew it. I was certain this time.

In that instant, my mechanical pencil turned into a knife, a small paring kitchen knife, but I didn't care. I used it. I struck his face and I struck it again. I struck a few more times in the face and I'm not sure how many passed, but soon I was aware my last two to three blows were to a dead face and I didn't feel remorse.

No, no remorse at all. No guilt.

I was safe. I was relieved.
I had survived. I had overcome.
I was at peace.

I didn't feel a soul leave the body.
I felt a monster without life.

It was then that my logic reappeared.
I had just killed a man.

My sister was no longer there.

This was all my doing.

I put him in a box.

I filled one side with his head. Pieces and cubes
of his head and I filled the other side with his
body. It was strange and amazing how this huge
man could fit in a tiny box once he had been cut
down.

I was about to close the box and dispose of it
without trace, but as I lifted the box off of the
floor to the countertop, an insurmountable
amount of dust and dirt poured in from an open
window in the room.

Was this a huge dust storm?
Was this a common thing?
Oh.. yeah, it was.

I quickly went to close it so the pieces of the
dead man wouldn't blow too far or out of the
room, but before I could do that I saw my sister
come in through the front door. My attention
quickly turned to the door as more dust and dirt
blew in, but she was getting covered in more! I
stretched out my arm to pull her into the house
and out of the storm, but as our hands grasped, a
bigger wave entered our house and affected all

the nearby houses as well. The worst was over, that was the last and strongest wave. Our neighborhood seemed snowed in, only it wasn't snow, it was sand.

We were all okay, but if I was now outside after being pulled out by the storm, then what became of that open box housing all those pieces of human flesh? Are they scattered about? All under these numerous dunes of sand? What happens when the sands get cleaned away?

Even worse, what if someone finds a piece??
Evidence will lead them right to me.
It was an act of defense.
I can still win this.
I won't go to jail.
What if I go to jail?
I know I killed someone, but that's not right.
What do I do?

It seems the house I am outside of reminds me a lot about a house on March Avenue.

I think I can leave. I think I can run away. No wait, I need to think more logically. I need sound reason to quietly kick in.

The dream breaks.

I'm in a new scene.

I'm sitting passenger side in a dark gray SUV,
who's the driver?
It's a woman and I know her, but I don't know
where we're going.
She's in a hurry, she says we need to go fast.
Does she know what I did?

I look out the windshield and the windshield
wipers are going. Are we snowed in? Why does
it look like winter now and why do I have a coat
on?
Gloves, a hat and is that a scarf she has on?

Something catches my eye from under her seat,
what is that? Is it slithering? So fast, it wraps up
and begins to cover the steering wheel. The
driver, apparently knew the snake and that it
lived there. Frustrated, she grabs the middle of
the snake and throws it down just a little too
harshly.
I understand we need to leave in a hurry and she
mumbles some sort of explanation about how its
normal and for me not to think too much about
her behavior towards it. I look down and see that
this snake is white with just a hint of green
within its lines.

That was the last thing I saw in the dream. According to a source, the color green in snakes would represent healing and personal growth, whereas white snakes in dreams usually symbolize a secret. The source went on to say, "It is possible that you are hiding something big and may not have shared it with anyone."

Estranged

Sigh.
Deep breath.
It's time.
I know it's not what you want.

This has to happen.
You have to do it.
For once and for all.
You're going to have to remember every detail
that you can.

It's been three years now and I know you
stopped sharing that story if you're sober. I can
count on my hands the number of people that
know a version of that story.

Heart beats three times the normal rate

Something that happened to me.
Something that I want to put out of my mind.

Two streams of tears come gliding

I, um... I don't talk to my dad anymore.

Heart pounding
New tears gliding
Sobs

Shouts, "I don't want to share this story!"

Crying inaudibly

Sobs audibly and recurrently
Two streams of tears meet to form one

This isn't easy for me.
My body remembers.
My hair stands up and I want to curl up into a
ball.

Dying from crying
Dying from trying

Dying from remembering. Every time I tell this
story, another part of me dies.

Sobs
Cries
Inaudible sob lasts ten seconds

I don't want to remember.
Why make me remember??

My hands are trembling.
I haven't stopped crying.

My therapist said it "re-traumatizes" me and that
I don't have to keep sharing. I wonder if I'll ever
stop crying.

People have cried.
People have gasped.
People have questioned.

People haven't understood.

To feel what I feel I would have to get you in
such a state of panic and confusion that I
wouldn't ever bear to seek.
But here I am and there I was.
My tears have dried and been re-wet.
For now the sobbing has stopped and yet, I still
feel this deep cavern of a dark sentiment.

I am trying to avoid it. I am creating space. I am
trying to keep peace. This storm, it blows me
away and I end up swirling in its midst for the
rest of my life. The winds have caught me and
they're making me dance around with them.

I'm scared.

Deep exhale

My therapist told me it's okay to breathe.
I catch three, but I don't release.
I'm gasping for air and these seconds feel longer
than they seem.
I'm frozen.
My leg will only shake.

Screams inaudibly for three seconds
Audibly and recurrently sobs three times

Screams inaudibly for three seconds again
*Audibly and recurrently sobs three times
again*

Sigh of exhaustion

We haven't even begun!

It's taken me three years to be able to write about
this. Three years..

This is a better start.
A calmer start.

I put the pen down,
I put the journal aside
I cried for a minute

In and out
Mostly out

It really pains me to relive this memory, this best
forgotten core memory. One that's lodged deep
in a root, deep in my heart's cavity. It feels like a
black hole, like a whirlpool. This dark storm,
this dark wind inside of me.

It can take me away if I let it, but I must hold
tight. You need to hear this tonight. It's not that I
want to tell you. It's not something I want you to
know. On the contrary, I wish I could hide this
away forever and keep it sealed tight. A secret
and it's one of my deepest, darkest ones alive.

Now, I question life. I question any and all
relationships. I question love. I question sex.

"My feet are dirty," she says with shame and
discomfort. I've walked through dirt and dust.
My feet have been tied and tried.

I don't like where I've been.

I know I'm still putting off the story.

I want you to know where I'm at right now. That
I'm okay and I've accomplished what I've

wanted in this life. I know I have. I've loved and
I've lost more times than I care to count. I have
good people around me and I follow their
advice. I need to share all of this with you so
you can understand my true blight.

I hold my breath.
My leg begins to shake.
I exhale, more, a lot more, than I inhale.
I think it's because I've kept a lot in.

I don't try. I just don't open the flood gates.

Maybe you're just waiting for me to get to the
good part.
There is no good part.

The little smile that quivers into a frown,
The nervous twitch that comes about.

I'm not laughing this time.
I begin crying this time.

I'm scared.

I don't want to start crying again because I know,
once I go back to the story, once I get back in

that state, I won't be able to get out as easily as I
slipped in.

This takes me back to that forgotten time.

I see the setting.
I hate the message.

I ponder how much to involve other names,
other places.

I don't know what to keep and/or what to keep
out. I fear I may fill up this whole journal and
drown out this fire red pen. I am not the bad
person in this story.

"You did what you felt you had to do in order to
survive," to quote a different therapist.

My therapist said this,
My therapist said that,
My sister said this,
My mom said that,
My cousin said this,
My friend said that,
My lover said this,
My stranger said that.

I guess I should tell you what happened.

Exhales sharply for twenty seconds

My dad had the sex talk with me today.

I had asked, while we were having brunch with
my aunt, if he would feel more at peace if I were
to get married.

He didn't say yes;
He didn't say no;
So, so.
His usual response.

He then began talking to my aunt, who is the
same age as me, about how when we're young
we don't think too much about our futures and
what we want in a spouse. He said we often go
off of looks and let fate decide the rest. This is
not the right way. One should get to know a
person first; their personality, their mindset, and
what they want out of life: their dreams. He also
prevailed to state a wide-known notion on the
basis of sex, as well, as the importance it carries
into happiness and ultimately, love. He said we
must satisfy each other and do it well; with time,
with care, with love and with devotion.

I agreed with him. Sex is very important when
going into marriage. I believe one should talk
about or already be in agreeance to what terms
will come about as well as the ones that are not
to be sought.

He told us a story of how he lost his virginity
when he had agreed to share rent with a woman
who came on to him. He said she was older than
him by almost a decade and that it took him by
surprise. He proceeded to uninvitedly tell us
about his first sexual experience. We were near
the end of the brunch, when he began to tell his
story; maybe he needs to release it?

Going back to his illicit story, he deemed it a
positive experience because he was instructed
and taught how to do everything right. I wasn't
too sure this adequate table talk, but dismissed
the thought seeing as we were all family and at
times, its best to speak with the truth
transparently. From what I gathered, his story
was quite perverse as he unknowingly described
someone who had just sexually groomed him. I
secretly felt pity for him as he described how
someone abused him.

He then proceeded to wrap up his story by
sounding astute. He told us the only reason why

someone would cheat on their spouse is if they are not getting satisfied in the bedroom. He turned his twisted logic to us. He asked, if we had a husband whom was no good in bed, would we be satisfied in the relationship? Quickly, he answered his own question, of course not. He wanted to back up his statement by informing us, of all the friends he's had that have cheated on their wives, one hundred percent of them were not satisfied in the bedroom.

Well, by now all the plates were gone and we were just there to talk. We saw fit to all go our separate ways. The tab was paid and the goodbyes were said. I started towards my truck, unlocked it and climbed in to the driver's seat. I heard my dad tell me to wait, that he was going to check the oil level and pass me a tool to carry in the truck.

I popped open the hood and waited for his green light. He closed the hood of the truck and came around to the driver's side door to place the tool along the door. I thought we were done, but he seemed to express interest in my earlier thought. "So you're thinking of marriage, is that right?"

My father and I don't have many meaningful conversations, but I thought this was one. I affirmed I was thinking about the possibility of marrying the guy I was with.

Crude, as always, he asked if I even knew how to wipe my own ass.

I took his rude comment with a grain of salt, and tried to lighten the mood by giving half a laugh and affirming I knew. He then asked if I had already slept with the guy I was with. I told him no. He interjected by asking if I was still a virgin, to which I also answered no. In that moment, I believed he was asking to gather more data and calculate some harsh realistic truth about how the guy I was with would view me in a disparaging light. I was not right.

I don't really want to remember the rest of this story.
He asked me if I'm satisfied with the man I chose.
He asked me if the man I chose can satisfy me.
He asked me if the man I chose has satisfied me.

It seemed like these questions happened at the same time.

A resounding yes, I had no doubts.

"With his mouth?," my dad asked.

I was so thrown. Um, I'm all for telling the truth, but where does the line get drawn?

He gave me this irritable facial expression and believed I was being a prude.

Unwantingly, I confirmed.

"And you?," He asked.

"No, not me."

He pondered for a few seconds and then asked, "But you know how to right?"

Thrown for a loop, am I supposed to tell my dad? It's pretty self-explanatory, I thought.

"Um, I guess," I answered almost in disgust.

He told me to scoot in to the driver's seat, that he just had to attempt to sit in and halfway close the driver side door while the truck next to us reversed out. Now he was sitting next to me and I was patiently waiting for the truck to leave. Now looking back I'm not sure if that truck was ever ignited or meaning to leave.

I guess I should say what I should say.

My dad tried to have sex with me.
He cornered me in his truck and he blocked my
escape.
He said many disgusting things, things I didn't
need to hear.
He offered me a new car in exchange for a
sexual affair.
He tried to brainwash me by telling me to think
of him as only a friend.
He said it didn't have to be weird, he could teach
me how.
He said there would be nothing wrong, unless I
were to get pregnant.

I never turned my head, I only looked straight
ahead.

I couldn't jump across to the passenger seat.
I couldn't go through the windshield.
He was blocking my one escape.

He kept telling me to think about it, that it would
be fun and that I would enjoy it.
I was frozen in fear, I kept declining every
disgusting offer.

He said we would keep it a secret, just
something between me and him.
After a while, I think he knew I was scared and
it was getting him off.
He mentioned the acne that I had and said it
stemmed from being sexually deprived.
I wanted the conversation to end, I wanted to
leave, I wanted to get out.
He said I didn't have to be so serious, he told me
to smile.
I gave a half smile hoping that this would be the
end.
But then he mentioned my dimples and how
they turn him on.
At that moment, I hated my dimples and I hated
every beautiful thing about me.
I hated my long hair, I hated my fit physique, I
hated the light color of my skin.
I hated my clothes for giving me shape, I hated
my persona for attracting this craze.
I rejected everything good about me hoping it
would save me.
I still couldn't turn my head, I was in a frozen
state.
The only thing that had mobility were my eyes
and I looked down. I looked over.
I could see a stain of pre cum on his crotch.
I could smell the putrid stench of his rot.
I looked away.

I didn't know what was going to happen.
I was afraid of what all could happen.
My heart racing out of my chest.
Save yourself.
Goosebumps that caused my hair to stand up,
An involuntary reaction to a false imprisonment.

He asked if he could kiss me in my dimples,
I said no.
He asked if he could kiss me on the cheek,
I said no.
He asked if he could kiss me on the lips,
I said no and managed to shake my head.
He then said he would leave,
I was relieved.
But then he asked for a hug before he left.

I was so confused.
I wanted him to leave.

I doubted he would take no for an answer.
I used to always hug him goodbye before today..
I gave in just so he could exit the truck.
I went in for a very quick hug so I could still get
away.

But he placed his hand near my shoulder and
started down my back,

I shrugged him off, but he wouldn't take a step
back.

I wanted to go.

He then took a step back.
Thank God.

But then he asked for me to give him a kiss on
the cheek.
We had never really done that before,
But I know of other fathers and daughters that
do that..
Out of fear, I obliged.

A quick peck and yes, I'm disgusted too,
But try to understand,
It was that or be trapped.

And then with the most deranged smile, he
asked for a kiss on the lips.
Bewildered, I stood my ground and I said no.
I looked away and now the door was shut.
I might make it.
He stood at the window and repeated his words.
"Think about it," he said with no shame.
I nodded my head just so I could get away.

Rage

Re: November 1, 2020

I wanted to go to the police when it all
happened.

I didn't know what to do.

Was it a crime to try?

It was disgusting for sure, but do you not care to
stop the guy behind such heinous attacks?

If he could do that to his daughter, what could he
do to another?

Are we not giving him the opportunity to try
again? With a different girl??

Are we giving him the opportunity to attempt
once again, but this time with a bigger rage? An
uncontrollable one?

That blood psycho rage.
That thrill of the pain.

They tell me to forgive him.

I don't know him.
I disown him.

I cut all attachments with that man.
That manic coward is nothing of mine.

Deprived degenerate,
I had hoped you had died.

I write in red and inflamed,
With blood boiling disdain,
I cannot stand the sight of that man.

I will not tame my roaring rage,
I will kill that man.

I have trained for that day.